DATE DUE

2 '06 Elmer		'07
SE 11 '06 Gilberto		46
SE 18 '06 Walter		40
MY 18 '07 Ivan velazquez		18
OC 10 '07 Oscar		117
AP 14 '08 Szymo e		110
JA 21 '09 sara	Potoso	115
NO 1 '09 vnaro	Range	110
OC 0 4 '09 aidi		118
5-9		

DEMCO 38-296

Beginning SOCCER

Coach Lori Coleman and these Richfield athletes were photographed for this book:

Rachel Ekholm,
Mandy Engberg,
Nate Evans-Winkel,
Angelina Gearhart,
Casey Herbert,
Ernest Julean,
Kacie Larson,
Vas Leckas,
Nichole Legus,
Jennifer Lenberg,
Neil Lenzen,
Elizabeth Petrik,
Marissa Santos,
Niels Sorensen,
Erick Stevens,
Wendy Walstrom.

Beginning
SOCCER

Julie Jensen

Adapted from
Lori Coleman's *Fundamental Soccer*

Photographs by Andy King

Lerner Publications Company ● Minneapolis

Library of Congress Cataloging-in-Publication Data

Jensen, Julie, 1957–
    Beginning soccer / by Julie Jensen ; photographs by Andy King ; adapted from Lori Coleman's Fundamental Soccer.
        p.   cm. — (Beginning sports)
    Includes bibliographical references and index.
    ISBN 0–8225–3501–7
    1. Soccer—Juvenile literature. I. King, Andy, ill.
II. Coleman, Lori. Fundamental soccer. III. Title. IV. Series.
GV943.25.J46   1994
796.334—dc20   94–37742

Manufactured in the United States of America
2 3 4 5 6 7 – HP – 02 01 00 99 98 97

The Beginning Sports series was designed in conjunction with the Fundamental Sports series to offer young athletes a basic understanding of various sports at two reading levels.

Photo Acknowledgments

Photographs are reproduced with the permission of: pp. 7, 8 (both), The Bettman Archive; p. 9, Allsport/ David Cannon; p. 27, © Jon Van Woerden; p. 58, Mark Backlund/Courtesy of Corner Kick Indoor Soccer Center, Maplewood, Minn.

Contents

Chapter 1

How This Game Got Started

Around the world, more people play and watch soccer than baseball, basketball, hockey, or football. But playing the game is even more exciting than watching! Soccer is a game of action. Players kick the ball around a large field. Other players dive to keep the ball from going into the goal.

Games like soccer were played all over the world long ago. A game much like modern soccer was first played in Derby, England, around A.D. 217. Romans ruled England

This ancient Greek vase shows a soccer player practicing.

7

Early Romans were soccer players.

then. The Romans probably passed along a game that they had started playing in earlier times.

In England, the Romans' game became known as football. The ball could be hit only with the feet, the body, or the head. Hands could not be used.

In 1823 some players changed the game. They used their hands to catch and throw the ball. Soccer players who liked the old rules formed the London

This drawing shows an American soccer match in 1890.

Football Association to protest using hands when playing. They called the original game "association football" to keep it separate from the new game, which was called rugby. The name was shortened to "assoc," and later to "soccer." But in some parts of the world, the game is still called football.

Soccer was the only football game in the United States until the 1870s. Then the American style of football became popular. In 1913 the United States Football Association was created to govern soccer. In 1945 the group's name was changed to the United States Soccer Federation (USSF). The USSF runs professional, amateur, and youth soccer programs. The USSF also organizes college teams, Olympic teams, and a number of other programs in the United States.

The Federation Internationale de Football Association (FIFA) controls soccer in 158 nations. Most soccer games in the world, including those played in the United States, are played by FIFA rules.

FIFA holds a very popular

West Germany won the World Cup in 1990.

tournament every four years. It is called the World Cup. All the countries that belong to FIFA can try to become one of the top 24 teams, which play in the tournament. The World Cup games were held in the United States in 1994.

Chapter 2

BASICS

Field of Play

A soccer field is a large rectangle. It can be from 100 to 130 yards long and from 50 to 100 yards wide. A **center line** divides the field in half. The **center circle** goes around the **center spot** in the middle of the field. The center spot is where the ball is first put in play to start a game.

A **goal**, 8 yards wide and 8 feet high, stands at each end of the field. A net is stretched between two **goalposts** on the sides and a **crossbar** across the top. Players try to kick the soccer ball into the opposing team's goal to score a point for their team.

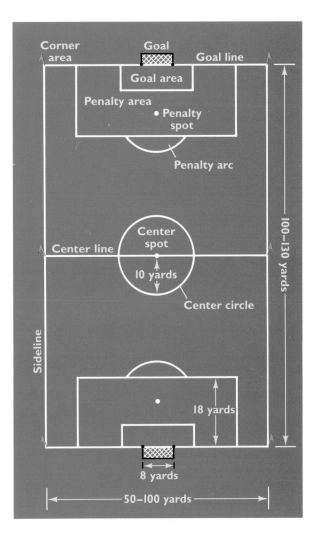

Equipment

Soccer shoes are very important. Shoes that fit poorly can hurt a player. Soccer shoes often have rubber or plastic cleats to give players solid footing.

Soccer players usually wear T-shirts for practice and jerseys for games. They also wear loose shorts, long socks, and shin guards to prevent injuries.

The **goalkeeper,** or goalie, stays in front of his or her team's goal. The goalkeeper is the only player who can touch the ball with his or her hands. The goalkeeper's uniform is a different color from his or her teammates' uniforms. Then opponents can tell which player is allowed to use his or her hands.

Balls

Soccer balls come in many colors and designs. Hand-sewn leather balls are soft and last longer than balls made from rubber or nylon. But rubber or nylon balls cost less.

An official soccer ball is 27 to 28 inches around and weighs 14 to 16 ounces. Young players can use smaller balls that are easier to kick.

Basic Moves

Dribbling

Soccer players move the ball on the field by **dribbling**. Kacie is dribbling while she jogs. Kacie touches the ball with either the laces or outside of her foot on each step. She uses both her left foot and her right foot to dribble.

Practice changing speeds and directions while you dribble. These skills help you control the ball during a game.

Nate is getting away from an opponent by using a fake. He keeps the ball close to him and under control. His body is between his opponent and the ball. Nate lunges one way so that his opponent also moves in that direction. Then Nate touches the ball with the bottom of his foot and rolls it the opposite way. He quickly dribbles in the opposite direction of his fake.

Inside of foot

Passing

A **pass** is the quickest way to move the ball on the soccer field. Players often stop the ball before passing it to a teammate.

To pass with the inside of her foot, Jessica places her non-kicking foot next to the ball. She keeps the ankle of her kicking foot firm as she strikes the ball. After she hits the ball, her kicking leg swings through. This gives the pass power.

Next, Jessica kicks the ball with the outside of her foot. Jessica keeps her ankle firm and follows through.

To hit the ball farther, Kristy passes with her **instep**. She hits the ball with the laces of her shoe and follows through.

Outside of foot

Instep of foot

You can use the heel of your foot to pass to a teammate behind you. Rachel is doing a **heel pass**. She puts her non-kicking foot next to the ball and swings back with her kicking foot. Her heel sends the ball behind her.

Sometimes players don't have time to stop the ball before passing it. Players then use the **one-touch pass** to receive a ball and pass it, all in the same motion. Rachel stands directly in the ball's path. As it reaches her, she swings her kicking foot to hit the ball in the direction she wants to pass.

A one-touch pass when the ball is in the air is called a **volley pass**.

Trapping

To **trap** the ball means to stop it and then put it in position so you can pass or dribble. You can trap with the foot, the thigh, the abdomen, or the chest.

To trap a ball on the ground with her foot, Kacie lifts her foot slightly off the ground. She stops the ball with the inside of that foot. Her leg moves back a little as her foot and the ball meet to keep the ball from bouncing away.

When the ball is just above the ground, it can be stopped using the instep. Kacie keeps her ankle firm. As she draws her foot back a little, the ball drops on the ground in front of her.

For a higher ball, Kacie hits the ball with her thigh. She drops her thigh a little when the ball hits to cushion it.

Next, Kacie traps a high ball by jumping up to meet it with her stomach. To trap even higher balls, players use the **chest trap**. To do this, Kristy gets in front of the ball. She uses her upper chest as a table on which the ball can land. As it hits, she leans her body forward and in the direction she wants it to fall.

Shooting

Like passing, **shooting** can be done using either foot. Mandy practices taking hard shots at the goal, using her instep to gain the most power.

Mandy runs up to the ball and places her nonkicking foot next to it. She strikes the ball with the laces of her kicking foot. Mandy keeps her ankle rigid and follows through with her kicking leg. She lands on her kicking foot.

Some players have trouble getting their foot underneath the ball to lift it into the air. Make sure you hit the ball with the instep. Strike the ball close to where it's touching the ground and follow through.

Heading

To do a **header,** Casey watches the ball and goes where it will land. She holds her arms out and leans back. When she hits the ball, she brings her shoulders forward and swings her arms back. She keeps her neck and chin firm, her eyes open, and her mouth closed. Casey hits the ball with her upper forehead, right at her hairline.

Soccer players use headers to score or pass. Headers don't hurt when they are done correctly. Remember, you are hitting the ball instead of letting the ball hit you.

Defense

When your team doesn't have the ball, you play **defense**.

Marking

Marissa stays close to the opponent she is **marking**. She also stays between that player and the goal that Marissa's team is defending. If the player that Marissa is marking has the ball, Marissa tries to force that player to move the ball where Marissa wants it to go.

Tackling

Soccer players also must be able to **tackle,** or take the ball away from an opponent.

Marissa forces the player she is marking to stop and turn. Marissa quickly kicks away the ball and gains control of it.

Goalkeeping

Goalkeepers must learn other skills for guarding their team's goal. Shots that would go in the goal if the goalie didn't stop them are called **shots on goal**.

The goalie must be able to reach, leap, and dive quickly. When waiting for action, the goalkeeper is in the **basic stance,** as Elizabeth is. Her knees are slightly bent, and her feet are about shoulder-width apart. Her arms and hands are raised and ready to stop any shot at the goal.

Positioning

The goalie can make the goal look smaller to a shooter by moving off the goal line into the field. This is called **positioning**. The goalkeeper then can tell where the shot will be aimed and try to block the ball.

Collecting

Goalies have to **collect,** or save, many rolling balls, bouncing balls, and high balls. To pick up rolling balls, Nichole keeps her feet together. Her hands are held out and slightly apart with the palms up. She leans over and scoops the ball up to her chest.

Keeper ! ! !

Tony Meola is one of the best-known goalkeepers in the United States. Meola and his friends in Kearny, New Jersey, grew up watching the New York Cosmos, a professional soccer team. Meola's family came to the United States from Italy.

Meola played baseball and soccer when he was growing up. In high school, he was an all-state baseball player and an all-state soccer player. He chose to play soccer at the University of Virginia. Later, he played for the U.S. team in the 1994 World Cup tournament. He made 38 saves in four games during the tournament.

Meola's friends call him "Meat" or "Meatball." He often comes off the goal line and stops an attack by intercepting a pass or stealing the ball from a dribbler. He can beat almost anyone in the air. Meola can punt the ball more than 80 yards downfield.

After the World Cup, Meola played professional soccer. He also acted in some Broadway shows.

When a shot is in the air, Elizabeth stands so that her body is between the ball and the goal. She holds her hands with the palms out and her thumbs together. Her hands form a W. Elizabeth catches the ball and hugs it to her body.

Sometimes Elizabeth leaps on one leg and brings up the other knee. She extends her arms to catch a high ball in midair.

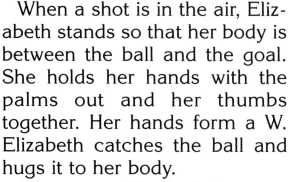

Sometimes the goalie has to punch the ball up over the goal or off to one side. To do this, Nichole jumps up with one knee raised. She punches the ball with a short, quick stroke.

Diving

Some exciting saves are made with **dives**. Diving is difficult and takes a lot of practice.

When first practicing, Rachel dives from her knees. A teammate tosses the ball to one side of her. As the ball approaches her, Rachel reaches out. She keeps her lower hand directly in the line of the ball's flight. She places her upper hand on top of the ball as it hits her lower hand. She holds the ball as she falls.

Next, Elizabeth dives from the basic stance position. As she takes off, Elizabeth stretches out her arms. She catches the ball and gets ready to hit the ground. Elizabeth rolls as she lands to soften her fall. She quickly gets up.

After a goalkeeper makes a save, he or she puts the ball back into play. The goalkeeper often throws the ball to a teammate.

To send the ball farther, the goalkeeper **punts**. The best punts are long but low. High-flying balls give the other team more time to react.

To punt, Elizabeth takes a couple of steps. She holds the ball over her kicking foot. She swings her leg and kicks through the ball.

Chapter 3

GAME TIME

Positions

There are 11 positions on a soccer team. One player is the goalkeeper. The other 10 are forwards, fullbacks, or midfielders.

Forwards often score the goals. They pass, help teammates with the ball, and dribble past defenders before they can shoot. Forwards who play near the sidelines are called **wings**.

Fullbacks play defense. They keep opponents away from their goal. Fullbacks mark players on the opposing team. They try to force opponents to make a bad pass or dribble.

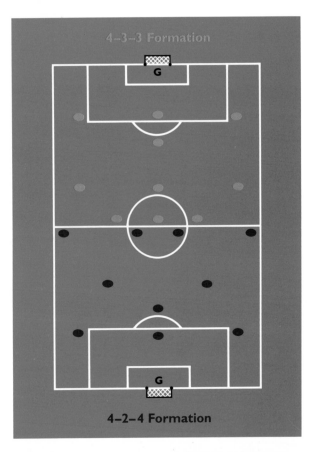

4–2–4 Formation

3–4–3 Formation

Midfielders help the forwards bring the ball down the field. They also help the fullbacks defend their goal.

Coaches use many formations of forwards, midfielders, and defenders. Some formations are shown on this page.

Rules

A goal is scored when the ball crosses the goal line between the goalposts and under the crossbar. Each goal scored is one point.

Games usually have two equal periods of playing time. Play begins with the **kickoff** at the center spot. The teams use a coin toss before the game to decide which team will kick off. The team that does not kick off at the beginning of the game kicks off at the start of the second period. After a team scores a goal, a player from the other team kicks off.

When the entire ball crosses the sideline or the goal line, the ball is out of bounds. Then it is out of play and must be returned to the field for play to continue.

If the ball goes out over a sideline, the team that did not send the ball out gets a **throw-in**. A player from that team throws the ball back into play.

If the ball goes out of bounds over the goal line and the team defending the goal last touched it, the other team gets a **corner kick**. The corner kick is kicked from one of the two **corner areas** on that end of the field. A player can score on a corner kick. Usually, however, the ball is kicked to a teammate in front of the goal.

When the ball goes out over the goal line and the team defending the goal did not touch it last, that team is given a **goal kick**. The ball is placed in the **goal area**, usually on the corner. The kicker kicks the ball to a teammate down the field.

Fouls

The referee's job in a game is to call major and minor violations of the rules. **Major violations** include pushing, tripping, holding, and **handball**. The referee calls handball if a player other than the goalkeeper uses his or

Throw-ins

The only time players other than the goalie can play the ball with their hands is on a throw-in. A defender or midfielder usually makes the throw.

The thrower watches to see which teammate is open to field the ball. The thrower must stand outside of the sideline with both feet on the ground. The thrower must use both hands to throw the ball over his or her head. The thrower wraps his or her hands around the ball with the thumbs touching. Then, the player brings the ball up over his or her head and steps forward. The player takes a second step. On the third step, the player throws the ball.

Yellow Card, Red Card

A referee decides when a player has committed a foul. Players must respect the referee. Players also must accept the calls the referee makes, even if the players don't agree.

If a player argues, uses bad language, or bothers an official or another player, the referee may show the player a **yellow card***. This is a warning to the player. If he or she doesn't follow the rules, the referee will show him or her a* **red card***. A red card means that player is out of the game.*

Drop Ball

When a player is injured, the referee has to stop play. Then the game is restarted with a drop ball. In a drop ball, one player from each team stands near the referee where the ball was last in play. The referee blows the whistle, drops the ball between the two players, and play begins.

her hands or arms to play the ball.

Minor violations of the rules include being **offside**. If a player is ahead of the ball in the attacking half of the field without at least two opponents between him or her and the goal, that player is offside. Offside is not called in corner kick, goal kick, or throw-in plays.

Other minor violations are **dangerous play** and **obstruction**. An example of dangerous play is a high kick that could hurt another player. Obstruction is intentionally blocking an opponent rather than trying to get the ball.

If the referee calls a major violation, the team that didn't commit the foul gets a **direct free kick**. For minor violations, the opposing team gets an **indirect free kick**. Both direct and indirect free kicks are taken from the spot where the rule was broken. All other players must be at least 10 yards away from the ball. A player can score a goal with a direct free kick. A player must kick the ball to a teammate on an indirect free kick.

If a player commits a major

violation in his or her team's penalty area, the opponents are given a **penalty kick**. The penalty kick is taken from the **penalty spot,** which is only 12 yards from the goal line. Only the goalie can defend the kick, so a goal is often scored!

Playing the Game

Let's see how the Reds and the Wildcats—teams in Richfield's city club—put the skills and rules of soccer into play. The Reds and Wildcats always start the season by playing against each other. The Wildcats won the coin toss, so they kick off.

Laura, a Wildcat forward, kicks the ball from the center spot to her teammate, Becky. Becky makes a long pass out to the wing, Melissa. A Reds full-back challenges Melissa and comes up with the ball. She sends the ball down to the Wild-cats' half of the field.

The Reds' right forward drib-bles down toward the Wildcats' goal. Chinda comes up to tackle for the ball. As she does, team-mate Marissa moves over to cover Chinda's territory. The ball is kicked out of bounds.

Special Tips

Know where your teammates and opponents are all the time. If you get the ball but weren't paying attention, you may not see an opponent who could steal the ball. If you do not know where your teammates are, you won't know where to pass the ball.

Teammates also should stay spread out over the field without bunching. If two or three teammates are in the same spot and one of them gets the ball, the other two aren't ready for a pass. Two or three teammates bunched in one place leave many open spaces on the field. If the ball goes to one of those spaces, an oppo-nent could easily control it.

Chinda moves back into position as left fullback. Marissa shifts back over to the center.

After about 15 minutes, some Wildcats are getting tired. Angelina and Xanara replace two of the midfielders on the field.

Jenny kicks a goal kick downfield to Kacie. She dribbles and then passes to Xanara. Xanara dribbles toward the Reds' goal. As she approaches the goal line,

Xanara kicks the ball up in front of the goal. Angelina jumps and heads the ball. She scores!

Now the Reds forwards move the ball toward the Wildcats' goal. One of the Reds players takes a shot on goal. Nichole jumps up to grab it. She punts the ball back down the field. Katie traps the ball with her stomach. She passes the ball back —a **support pass**—to Emily.

The referee blows his whistle. Halftime already! Coach tells the players to keep spread out on the field. If they all go for the ball, there is no one open to take a pass. "Make sure you call for balls and for passes," the coach reminds them.

Soon after the second half begins, Angelina gets the ball near the middle of the field. Becky sprints toward the Reds' goal and Angelina passes to her. The referee blows his whistle. Becky was past all of the defenders before she received the pass. Because she was offside, the Reds get a free kick.

Later in the game, Angelina kicks the ball downfield to Becky again. This time, a defender and the goalie are between Becky and the goal. Becky sprints downfield with the ball. She fakes a shot. The defender moves to block the shot and Becky dribbles the ball around her. The goalie comes off the goal line and starts toward Becky. Becky aims and shoots the ball to the lower right corner—another score!

Now the Reds quickly bring the ball toward the Wildcats' goal. While playing defense, Marissa accidentally kicks the ball out past the goal line. The Reds get a corner kick.

The corner kick is a high ball right in front of the goal. A Red forward meets the ball in the air with her foot, volleying it right past Nichole into the goal. The Reds have a point.

But soon the referee blows his whistle one last time, and the game is over. The Wildcats win! The Reds and Wildcats line up and shake hands.

Total Soccer

All players attack and defend in total soccer. For one thing, that means teammates can fill in at one another's positions.

For example, a forward may see that a fullback on her team is challenging an opposing player for the ball. Instead of waiting upfield, the forward hustles back to cover at defense in case the fullback gets beat.

Players also can switch positions on offense. If a fullback has the ball and sees that his best option is to dribble the ball instead of passing, he does so. He knows that a teammate will cover his position until he gets back.

PRACTICE, PRACTICE

Richfield boys and girls teams practice on the days they don't play games. Each practice session has some stretching, running, and drills.

First, the boys dribble around the field to warm up their muscles. Then, they get into a circle for stretching. They stretch all the muscles in their legs, backs, arms, and necks.

After stretching, Niels and Neil lead the players in some exercises. With his feet together, Neil stands next to a ball. He jumps over it, keeping his feet together. He and his teammates do this 25 times.

43

Next, Neil jumps forward and backward over the ball. The Reds do this 25 times, too. These exercises help improve their coordination and increase their leg strength.

Now the boys get into pairs. Each player links ankles with his partner while in sit-up position. The partners pass a soccer ball back and forth as they do sit-ups. The player with the ball must touch it to the ground behind his head as he lays back after each sit-up. This exercise builds the players' stomach muscles.

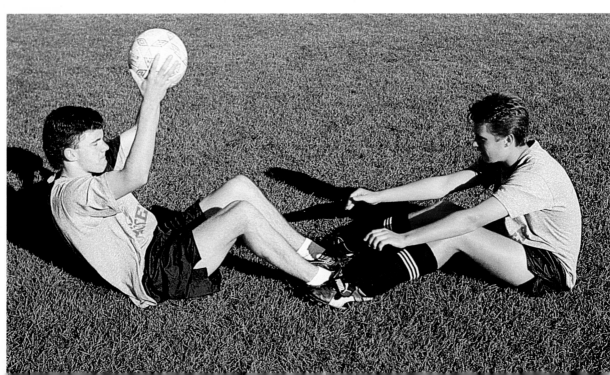

Erick leads the next exercise, his favorite. First, he throws the ball up, as high and as straight as he can. Then Erick quickly does a somersault, bounces up, and catches the ball.

Sprinting helps make the Reds faster. Jogging helps build up their endurance. One drill uses both jogging and sprinting. The boys jog around the field in single file. The last one in the line sprints to the front of the line. He yells for the next person to go. The last player in line again sprints to the front as the line of players jogs along.

Drills and Skills Training

There is one drill that soccer players can do any time. All a player needs is a ball. That drill is **juggling**.

The idea is to keep the ball from touching the ground. You can use your feet, thighs, head, and any other part of your body except your hands and arms.

When Niels juggles, he keeps track of the number of touches he makes before the ball hits the ground.

Dribbling drills also improve a player's ball-handling skills. In one drill, Coach Smith sets up a line of cones a couple of steps apart from one another. Neil starts at the first cone. He dribbles the ball around each of the cones. After Neil has started, the next player begins dribbling around the cones.

In another drill, each player gets a ball. The players stand inside the center circle on the field. When Coach Smith blows his whistle, the players dribble around the circle. They keep their heads up so that they don't run into each other. First, Coach Smith calls out "Inside!" Then each player touches his ball twice with the inside of his foot. The players sprint for a couple of steps before returning to a jogging dribble. Then the coach calls "Outside!" The players do the same routine, but touch the ball with the outside of the foot. When Coach Smith yells out "Touch!" each player touches his ball with the bottom of his foot. When he yells "Switch!" they quickly change direction.

In the pass weave drill, Rachel, Jenny, and Wendy jog side by side about 10 yards apart. Jenny passes the ball to Rachel. Jenny takes Rachel's place as Rachel dribbles toward the center. Rachel passes to Wendy and goes to the left. Wendy brings the ball to the center and passes to Jenny. They jog and pass until they get to the end of the field.

In another passing drill, one player stands in the middle of a circle of passers. Everyone in the circle passes a ball around. The player in the middle tries to get the ball. When he does, he takes the place of the player whose pass he blocked and that player goes in the middle.

One-on-one play is another good way to practice skills. Niels and Neil are practicing shadowing. In this drill, Niels has the ball. Neil marks him closely from behind. He tries to keep Niels from dribbling in the direction Niels wants to go.

There's another way to practice one-on-one play. A goalkeeper stands in front of the goal. The other players line up in one of two lines. One line is at the edge of the goal. The other is at the top of the goal area.

Each player behind the end-line has a ball. The first player in that line passes the ball to the first person in the other line. The player receiving the pass traps the ball. Then that player dribbles in and shoots. The player who passed the ball runs to play defense against the shooter.

Chapter 5

RAZZLE DAZZLE

With practice, soccer players become better. And the more a team plays together, the better the team becomes. Practice also helps players do more difficult moves.

Good ball-handling skills mean a player will be able to dribble past opponents in a game. Good ball handlers are creative and use a variety of moves to go in any direction.

You can see many spectacular moves in advanced soccer matches. With practice, you can also do them.

Pro Soccer in the United States

Many American players would like to be able to earn a living playing soccer in the United States. But professional soccer leagues haven't done well in the United States.

The United States Interregional Soccer League (USISL) is hoping to change that. In 1986, the USISL began with five teams. Amateur, or unpaid, players played on the same team as professional, or paid, players. As of 1996, the USISL had about 120 teams. They are split into two professional leagues and three amateur leagues. The professional leagues have about 57 teams. The amateur leagues have about 65 teams. They include a women's league and an indoor league.

Diving Header

One advanced skill is the **diving header**. By diving to head the ball, you can hit it quickly and with power. Players often learn how to do diving headers in a sand pit. There they have a soft surface on which to land.

Vas and Nate are practicing diving headers. Vas tosses the ball as Nate runs to the goal. Nate dives forward with his arms out to the sides. He hits the ball with his forehead. Nate keeps his neck firm and his eyes open. He lands with his arms first on the ground to soften the impact. Then it is Vas's turn to dive.

Sliding Tackle

Another exciting move is the **sliding tackle**. A player must hit the ball, not the opponent. Casey focuses on the ball when she slide tackles. When she is close to it, Casey tucks her right leg under. She thrusts her left leg out as she slides to the ball. Just before her opponent gets a foot on the ball, Casey kicks it out of her opponent's reach.

Scissors Kick

Nate is doing a **scissors kick**, or **bicycle kick**. Nate jumps up. As his kicking foot is about to hit the ball, he thrusts his other foot back and down. After he hits the ball, Nate cushions his fall with his arms.

Indoors

Indoor soccer uses the same skills, but the game is a bit different from soccer played outdoors. For one thing, an indoor soccer field is 52 yards long and 36 yards wide. The goals are 12 feet wide and 6½ feet high. Because the playing space is so much smaller, each team has just six players—including the goalkeeper—on the field at a time.

With less room, players must think and react faster. Teams win with short, quick, accurate passes and good ball control.

There are also some different rules. When the ball goes out of bounds over a sideline, the team that didn't last touch it gets a **kick in**. A player sets the ball on the sideline at the point where it went out and kicks it back into play.

If one team kicks the ball out of play across the goal line it is defending, the other team gets a corner kick.

If the attacking team kicks the ball out across the goal line, the other team gets the ball. The goalie must throw the ball back into play.

The goalkeeper can never throw, punt, or drop-kick the ball past the halfway line. If the goalkeeper does play the ball past the center line, the other team gets an indirect free kick from the center line.

SOCCER TALK

basic stance: The standing position from which a player—especially a goalkeeper—can most easily make a move for the ball. In the basic stance, the goalkeeper is on the toes, with the knees slightly bent and the arms out.

bicycle kick: An aerial kick done while jumping up and backwards in a back somersault motion. Also called a **scissors kick**.

center circle: The circle at the center of the field with a radius of 10 yards from the center spot.

center line: The line through the middle of the field that divides the field in half.

center spot: The spot in the center of the field from which kickoffs are taken.

chest trap: The technique of stopping a ball in the air by using the chest.

collecting: The technique of receiving a ground or airborne ball and controlling it before putting it in play. Also called trapping.

corner area: The arc around each of the field's four corners. Corner kicks are taken from these areas.

corner kick: A direct free kick taken from the corner area after the ball is played out of bounds past the goal line by the defending team.

crossbar: A bar, 8 yards long, that forms the top boundary of the goal and to which the net is attached.

dangerous play: A minor violation, such as a high kick, that could cause injury to another player.

defense: The type of play used when the ball is on a team's own side of the field. On defense, players work to move the ball away from their own goal.

direct free kick: A free kick that can score a goal without the ball being touched first by another player. A direct free kick is awarded to a team when the opposing team commits a major violation, such as a handball.

diving: A technique used mainly by goalkeepers in an attempt to save a shot on goal.

diving header: A way to hit the ball powerfully with the head. The diving header is an advanced move.

dribbling: Running while touching the ball with the feet to keep it in control and moving along with the player.

forward: A player position, mainly used for offense. Forwards are usually goal scorers.

fullback: A player position, mainly used for defense. Fullbacks work with the goalkeeper to keep the opposing team from shooting on goal and scoring.

goal: The area between the goalposts and the crossbar. A team scores a point when the ball is completely inside the opponents' goal.

goal area: The area immediately around the goal from which goal kicks are taken. The goal area measures 6 yards by 20 yards.

goalkeeper: One of a team's 11 players on the field. As the primary defender of the team's goal, the goalkeeper is the only player who can use his or her hands to play the ball (except for a throw-in).

goal kick: A free kick taken by the team defending the goal after the ball goes out of bounds and was last touched by the opposing team. The goal kick is taken from the goal area.

goalposts: The two bars, both 8 feet tall, that define the boundaries of the goal and to which the crossbar and netting are attached.

handball: The use of the hands by anyone other than the goalkeeper to play the ball. Handball is a major violation.

header: A technique used to play the ball by hitting it with the forehead, near the hairline.

heel pass: A way to pass the ball back to a player in a support position. Instead of turning, the passer stops the ball and hits it back with the heel.

indirect free kick: A free kick that cannot score a goal without first touching another player. Indirect free kicks are awarded when the opposing team commits a minor violation, such as offside.

instep: The part of the foot covered by the shoelaces. The instep is used to make powerful kicks.

juggling: The technique of keeping the ball in the air by making touches with the feet, thighs, chest, and head. Juggling is a good way to improve ball control.

kick-in: In indoor soccer, the method of returning the ball into play after it goes out of bounds over a sideline. A player kicks from the spot where the ball went out of play.

kickoff: The way to begin play at the start of the game, after halftime, and after a goal is scored. The ball is played from the center spot and must rotate one full turn before it is touched by another player. During kickoff, opposing players must stay outside of the center circle.

major violation: A foul for which the opposing team is awarded a direct free kick. Major violations include handball, pushing, holding, and tripping.

marking: The technique of defending in which a player stays close to an opponent, guarding against an attack by the opponent.

midfielder: A position on the field between the forwards and the full-backs. Midfielders must play both offense and defense.

minor violation: A foul for which the opposing team is awarded an indirect free kick. Minor violations include dangerous play, obstruction, and offside.

obstruction: A deliberate attempt to block an opponent's movement instead of playing the ball.

offside: A player is offside if he or she is on the opponents' half of the field with only one opponent between the player and the goal when the ball is played. Offside is a minor violation.

one-touch pass: A technique used to receive the ball and pass it on with only one touch.

passing: Playing the ball to a teammate by kicking or heading. Passing is one of the most important ways of moving the ball on the field.

penalty arc: The arc connected to the penalty area, outside of which players must stand during a penalty kick.

penalty area: The large area marked in front of each goal, which surrounds the goal area. The goalkeeper may use the hands to play the ball only within this area. If a major violation is committed within the penalty area by the defending team, the opposing team is awarded a penalty kick.

penalty kick: A direct free kick taken after a major violation is committed by the opponents in their own penalty area. The penalty kick is taken from the penalty spot.

penalty spot: The spot from which penalty kicks are taken. The penalty spot is located 12 yards in front of the center of the goal.

positioning: The technique used by a goalkeeper to block the goal from the opponent. By moving into certain positions in front of the goal, the goalie can cut off the angles open to a shooter.

punt: One of the ways a goalkeeper may put the ball into play after making a save. The goalie holds the ball out in front and makes an aerial kick with his or her laces. Punting enables the goalkeeper to send the ball far downfield.

red card: The referee's signal to inform a player that he or she is expelled from the game.

scissors kick: An aerial kick done while jumping up and backwards in a back somersault motion. Also called a **bicycle kick**.

shooting: An attempt to score a goal by kicking, heading, or otherwise touching the ball to send it toward the goal.

shot on goal: An attempt to score a goal that requires a save.

sliding tackle: An advanced defensive technique used to quickly take the ball away from an opponent by sliding.

support pass: A pass to a teammate positioned behind the passer.

tackle: A defensive technique used to take the ball away from an opponent.

throw-in: The method of returning the ball into play after it has been played out of bounds over the sideline by an opponent.

trapping: Coming into possession of the ball by collecting and controlling it.

volley pass: A one-touch pass made in the air.

wing: A player in the outside forward position.

yellow card: A referee's warning signal to a player to inform him or her that another misconduct will result in being expelled from the game.

FURTHER READING

Arnold, Caroline. *Soccer: From Neighborhood Play to the World Cup*. New York: Franklin Watts, 1991.

Chyzowych, Walter. *The Official Soccer Book*. Chicago, Illinois: Rand McNally & Company, 1978.

LaBlanc, Michael and Richard Henshaw. *The World Encyclopedia of Soccer*. Detroit, Michigan: Gale Research, 1994.

Luxbacher, Joseph A. and Gene Klein. *The Soccer Goalkeeper*. Champaign, Illinois: Human Kinetics Publishers, 1993.

Morrison, Ian. *The Hamlyn Encyclopedia of Soccer*. London: The Hamlyn Publishing Group, Ltd., 1989.

Yannis, Alex. *Inside Soccer*. New York: McGraw-Hill, Inc., 1980.

FOR MORE INFORMATION

Intercollegiate Soccer Association of America
1821 Sunny Drive
St. Louis, MO 63122

United States Soccer Federation (USSF) National Office
1801-1811 S. Prairie Avenue
Chicago, IL 60616

U. S. Youth Soccer Association
899 Presidential Drive
Suite 117
Richardson, TX 75082

INDEX